Peace and Joy

Scott Curran

Peace and Joy

To you, my friend in God.

Contents

Introduction

Peace and Joy is a collection of two previously-published kindle ebooks:

How to be Peaceful

How to be Joyful

Both books are written from the point of view of God speaking to you and both include references to relevant verses of scripture.

The books are available individually in ebook format or in this two-book collection called Peace and Joy, which is available both in ebook format and in paperback.

Peace and joy be with you, my spiritual friend.

How to Be Peaceful

How to Be Peaceful

To you -- my friend in God.

Contents

Introduction

How to Be Peaceful is about leaving everything to God. It reminds us that God is in control and that whatever is and whatever happens is what's best. It's written from the point of view of God speaking to you. Each chapter includes references to relevant verses of scripture. Peace be with you, my spiritual friend.

Chapter 1 - Live in the Present Moment

To be peaceful, live in the present moment.

All that happens is for your good.

Don't worry about your life. Don't worry about tomorrow. There's nothing to worry about.

It's always now. That's all there is.

You're in me. I'm in you.

I'm the Life of your Life, the Consciousness of your Consciousness.

No worries. No regrets.

Let any concerns you have dissolve in the ocean of my grace.

No matter how chaotic or difficult things appear to be, you have my peace within you. I've given it to you as a gift.

Where you are at this moment is precisely where you're supposed to be. Every detail of your life is exactly the way it's meant to be, and it's all for the best.

There's something about every person, place, thing, condition and situation that can bring you to a deeper spiritual awareness.

Be mindful of me in this present moment.

You have my peace -- right now.

Be conscious of my peace within you.

My peace fills you to overflowing. It then flows over to others, often without you even being aware of it.

Philippians 2:13 Matthew 6:34 John 14:27 Luke 12:22-34

Chapter 2 - Have Humility

To be peaceful, have humility.

Who are you trying to impress? Why? You don't have to impress anyone. So relax.

Be content to be last.

Be a servant.

Your humility toward others shows your humility toward me.

Every one is special. So there's nothing special about being special.

It doesn't matter if someone approves or disapproves of you.

You are who you are, by my grace.

If you're praised or insulted, applauded or ignored, what does it matter?

The things of this world don't matter.

Apart from me, you and all creatures are nothing.

Quit trying to control things. You aren't in control. I am.

I'm in control of everything, and that includes every detail of your life.

Abandon yourself to my will and be at peace.

I love you and I'm looking after things.

Trust in me, and be at peace with whatever is and whatever happens.

Luke 14:7-11 1 Corinthians 15:10 Mark 10:35-45 John 15:5
Jeremiah 10:23

Chapter 3 - Go Slow

To be peaceful, go slow.

What's the big hurry?

Be mindful of me in all that you do.

I'm looking after everything.

When you're going somewhere, leave early so you don't feel rushed.

If, for some reason, you're late, then you're late. Life will go on.

Don't book a lot of things if you don't have to.

Walk slow, talk slow, drive slow, think slow.

Do everything in a peaceful way.

I go before you and I smooth the path ahead.

Take time for solitude.

Inside or outside, sit quietly for a while.

Go for a leisurely walk outside.

Look at the flowers. Aren't they beautiful?

Take time to contemplate, to pray or to read something spiritually uplifting.

Easy does it.

Be at peace in the awareness of my presence.

Isaiah 45:2 Luke 10:38-42 Luke 19:28-32 Luke 5:16

Chapter 4 - Be Kind

To be peaceful, be kind.

When you're mean to someone, you don't experience peacefulness.

Treat others the way you'd like to be treated.

There's only One Life and it's being manifested in various forms.

What you do to others you do to me, and to your real self, because I'm the One Life within everyone.

When you hurt others, you're hurting yourself.

When you love others, you're loving yourself.

When you love yourself, you're loving others.

When you're kind to others, you're peaceful, because you're acting in accord with your true nature.

Be kind to the wicked and ungrateful.

Be kind to outcasts. Be kind to everyone.

Mourn with those who mourn. Rejoice with those who are celebrating.

Do acts of kindness.

Be considerate and kind -- and enjoy peace of mind.

Ephesians 4:32 1 Corinthians 13:4 Proverbs 11:17 1 John 3:18 Luke 6:27-36

Chapter 5 - Have Gratitude

To be peaceful, have gratitude.

Consider how lavishly you've been blessed.

In every occurrence, see me.

Be thankful for everything, even things that seem to be destroying you. Things that seem to be crucifying your ego self are bringing you to a new life in me.

When you're ignored or reviled, rejoice and give praise to me.

Appreciate what you have.

Whatever is happening, in every detail of your life, moment by moment, is my will for you, and what I will is always what is best.

If you're in good health, be thankful.   If you're ill, be thankful. Be thankful regardless.

Everything that occurs is my loving will for you.

Be grateful, whether I give or take away.   Nothing ever belonged to you anyway.

Give thanks in all circumstances.

Give thanks for everything as it is right now.

1 Thessalonians 5:18 Mark 8:6 Matthew 5:11-12 Colossians 3:15 Ephesians 5:19-20

Chapter 6 - Know That You're Forgiven and Forgive Others

To be peaceful, know that you're forgiven and forgive others.

Offer up your broken and contrite heart to me.

My love is greater than your sin.

Trust in my grace.

Love doesn't keep a record of wrongs.

Let yourself and others off the hook.

Accept my forgiveness and forgive yourself too.

Your sins are forgiven. Go in peace.

Be merciful, just as I'm merciful.

Forgive as I've forgiven you.

Luke 6:36 Psalm 51:17 1 Corinthians 13:5 1 Peter 3:18 1 Peter 4:8 1 Timothy 4:10 1 John 1:9 Luke 7:48-50

Chapter 7 - Use Words Wisely

Don't talk much.

The more you talk, the more likely you are to slip into boasting, gossip, deception, detraction, expressions of anger and other sins. So keep a tight rein on your tongue.

Don't complain. When you complain, you're saying that you know better than I do what's best. You don't. So be quiet.

Don't be critical of people. At some level, every one is doing the best they can.

Speak words that encourage others.

Listen carefully and be slow to speak.

Your words reveal what's in your heart.

Talking can be used not only to reveal, but also to conceal. It can be used as a smokescreen to hide shame. Just be quiet and be real.

Be thoughtful and considerate when speaking.

Blessed are peacemakers. Let your words bring peace.

Proverbs 10:19 James 1:19 James 1:26 Luke 6:45 Matthew 5:9 Colossians 4:6

Chapter 8 - Love

To be peaceful, know my love for you, and love others.

I'm Love. I made you.

I love you -- exactly as you are.

I'm delighted with you.

There's no fear in love. Perfect love drives away all fear.

As light banishes darkness, so does love banish fear.

Love whatever is, just the way it is.

Love whatever happens, just the way it happens.

Love others, just as they are.

Love yourself, just as you are.

Love lifts you out of delusion.

Love is Reality. It's the only Reality.

You don't have to like everyone, but do love them.

Love yourself and others as I love you.

You show your love for me by loving others.

Love isn't a feeling or an emotion. Love is a choice.

Choose to love, and live in peace.

Matthew 22:36-40   John 13:34   1 John 4:18   Matthew 5:44
John 15:17   Galatians 5:14   Ephesians 5:2   1 John 4:7
Matthew 3:16-17

Chapter 9 - Have Faith

To be peaceful, have faith in me.

Look through appearances. See me in all that is and all that happens.

Trust in me, always and everywhere, in every aspect of your life.

I keep you in perfect peace. Just keep your mind on me and trust me.

Whatever happens or doesn't happen is perfect.

I go before you and behind.

Trust in my love and mercy, now and at the hour of your death.

Surrender yourself to me and be free.

I'm with you in times of suffering and in times of ease. I'm with you always.

I'm Love and I'm all powerful. I'm in control of everything. Whatever occurs is my loving will for you. So why worry about anything? Trust in me and be filled with peace.

Proverbs 3:5-6 1 Peter 5:10 James 1:2-4 Romans 8:18 Luke 14:27 Matthew 28:20

Chapter 10 - Have a Sense of Wonder

To be peaceful, have a sense of wonder.

You're living in the midst of the miraculous every day.

Consider your being. What a wonderful creation you are!

Look at the birds and the flowers. Aren't they amazing?

Gaze into the blue sky. How peaceful it is.

The whole earth is filled with my glory.

Think of the wonderful people you've known, and the many kindnesses you've been shown.

Look at how the enchanting moonlight dances upon the river at night.

Enjoy the beauty of flowers and trees, and the refreshing feeling of a morning breeze.

Delight in the fragrance of freshly-cut grass, and the aroma of the earth after a shower has passed.

Be thankful for music and dancing and laughter and fun, and delight in the mystery of being one with the One.

I'm everywhere -- and I'm in you. I'm in everything - and beyond everything too.

I've put eternity into your heart.

Psalm 139:13-14 Isaiah 6:3 Jeremiah 23:23-24 Ecclesiastes 3:11

Chapter 11 - Accept All, Judge Nothing

To be peaceful, accept all and judge nothing.

Everything is how it's meant to be.

Accept others as you'd like to be accepted.

Accept others as I accept you.

Every event in your life, every person you come across, every place you are, moment by moment, year by year, is ordained by me.

Each person in your life -- each member of your family, each person you've worked with and socialized with, each person who lives on your street, each person standing in line with you at the store -- is meant to be in that role in your life, and you are meant to be in that role in theirs.

Don't judge anyone or anything.

They are who they are. It is what it is.

Look through the appearances and see the Reality -- Me.

Don't get upset about getting upset.   Don't get angry about getting angry. It's part of being human. I'm working in you according to my good purpose. So leave everything to me, and you be at peace.

You and others are all weak and weird in one way or another, so acknowledge that and accept each other.

Don't try to change anything outside of yourself or within yourself.

Apart from me, you can do nothing.

Not by might or power, but by my spirit.

Abandon yourself to me, and my unexplainable peace will rule your heart and mind.

Luke 6:37 Romans 15:7 Philippians 2:13 1 John 7:24 John 15:5 Philippians 4:7 Zechariah 4:6

Chapter 12 - Keep Things in Perspective

To be peaceful, keep things in perspective.

Your earthly life is like a mist -- it's seen for a little while and then it vanishes.

The sun is just one of trillions of stars. The earth is just one of trillions of planets.

There are billions of people on Earth. You're one of them.

In a little over a hundred years, all of the people who are now on Earth will be gone.

With me, a day is like a thousand years and a thousand years are like a day.

You have my peace, now and always. It's within you. To access it, be conscious of it. My peace isn't the same as what the world gives. The peace I've given you isn't based on what's happening around you. It transcends circumstances.

In this world you'll have trouble. But take heart. I've overcome the world, and I'm the essence of who you are.

In me, you are not of the world anymore than I am of the world.

You're a citizen of heaven.

Abandon yourself to me, trusting in my love and mercy.

One day there'll be no more death, sorrow, crying or pain. You'll have departed from the physical plane.

James 4:14   2 Peter 3:8   Psalm 103:15-16   John 17:14
Philippians 3:20 Revelation 21:4

Chapter 13 - No Resistance

To be peaceful, offer no resistance.

Don't resist an evil person.

If someone slaps you on one cheek, offer the other also.

If someone wants to take your shirt, let him have your coat too.

If you're forced to go a mile, go two miles.

Give to someone who asks, and don't turn away from someone who wants to borrow from you.

You don't overcome evil with evil. Overcome evil with good.

Be compassionate and humble.

Don't repay evil with evil or insult with insult. Instead, bless the person, and you'll be blessed by me.

Love your enemies. Pray for them. In doing that, you'll be acting in harmony with what you are -- a child of light.

What is, is. What happens, happens.

There are no coincidences. Nothing happens by chance.

Trust in me, go with the flow and be peaceful.

Matthew 5:39-48 Romans 12:17 Romans 12:21 1 Peter 3:9

Chapter 14 - Be Who You Are

To be peaceful, be who you are. Be your real self.

I live in, through and as you.

I'm Life.

You are in me and I am in you.

I'm the essence of who you are. I'm your real self. I'm expressing myself as you.

Rise beyond the brainwashing and conditioning of the world. Be changed by a complete change of your mind.

Put on the new self -- your real self.

I'm the Life of your Life, now and forever.

Be dead to your old self and be alive in me.

Become nothing, and be who you really are.

Be born anew in your consciousness and know -- you are spirit.

Flesh gives birth to flesh. Spirit gives birth to spirit.

The Spirit gives life. The flesh doesn't count for anything.

We are one.

In me, you're peaceful.

Colossians 3:1-3   Mark 8:36   Ephesians 4:24   John 14:20
Galatians 2:20 Matthew 28:20 John 3:3-8 John 6:63 John 17:22

Amen.

How to Be Joyful

How to Be Joyful

To you -- my friend in God.

Contents

Introduction

How to Be Joyful is about forgetting our self and trusting God. It's about seeing God's perfect will in all that is and all that happens. It's written from the point of view of God speaking to you. Each chapter includes references to relevant passages of scripture. Joy be with you, my spiritual friend.

Chapter 1 - Be Humble

To be joyful, be humble.

Forget yourself. Lose yourself in me. That's humility.

Have the same attitude as Christ Jesus.

Christ demonstrated the power of humility.

Humble yourself before me. I'll lift you up.

Your humility before me is shown by how you act with other people.

When people insult you, you're blessed. If an insult bothers you, it's showing you that you need more humility. An insult is aimed at your pride. If you had become nothing, you wouldn't care. An insult couldn't affect you if you weren't there.

I'll exalt you in my way at the right time.

In humility, you have wisdom.

The deeper you enter into humility, the more you're a conduit of my glory.

Egotism is a self-made prison. Humility is the key that sets you free.

In me, you're gentle and humble of heart.

In humility, you have joy.

The less of you, the more of me.

I'm telling you these things so that you'll know my joy within you and so that your joy will be complete.

Mark 8:35   Philippians 2:5-12   James 4:10   Titus 3:2
Matthew 5:11   1 Peter 5:6   Proverbs 11:2   Isaiah 29:19
Matthew 11:29 John 15:11

Chapter 2 - Acknowledge Your Sorrows

To be joyful, acknowledge your sorrows.

I comfort you when you mourn.

It's not 'unspiritual' to experience sadness.

Come to me -- and I'll give you rest.

I'm close to you when you're broken-hearted.

I restore you when you feel like your spirit's been crushed.

Offer up your broken heart to me.

I'll never leave you. I'll never forsake you.

I'm with you in your sufferings and your sorrows.

I'm with you always.

I'm looking after you.

Cast all your worries on me.

Apart from me, you can do nothing.

In your weakness, turn to me.

Acknowledge that you're powerless.

My spirit in your inner being renews you, strengthens you and guides you.

Abandon yourself to me and be at peace.

Be joyful in all circumstances.

Matthew 5:4   John 11:35   Matthew 11:28   Psalm 34:18
Psalm 147:3 Psalm 51:17 John 14:1 Mark 15:34 Hebrews
13:5 Matthew 28:20 1 Peter 5:7 John 15:5 2 Corinthians
12:9

Chapter 3 - Be Thankful

To be joyful, be thankful.

Give thanks to me for everything.

I say to give thanks to me for everything not because I need your thanks, but because it benefits you.

Having an attitude of gratitude shows that you trust me.

My loving will is revealed in all that happens, regardless of how it appears to your senses.

Having a grateful heart makes you joyful.

Be thankful not only for things that seem good, but also for apparent disasters and everyday annoyances.

Give thanks for delays, for the burnt toast, for the plumbing problem, for illnesses, for injuries, for difficult people, for someone's hurtful remark, for being ignored -- for everything.

All that occurs is for your good, even if, to your mortal mind, it seems terrible.

Trust in my divine providence.

Give praise continually.

Say, 'Thank you, God,' silently or audibly, perhaps a hundred or a thousand times each day.

Give thanks in all circumstances, pray continually and be joyful always!

1 Thessalonians 5:16-18   Ephesians 5:19-20   Colossians 3:15-17 Colossians 2:7

Chapter 4 - Keep it Simple

To be joyful, keep it simple.

You don't need a lot of stuff.

If you have stuff you don't need, get rid of it!

Be joyful in the present moment.

My infinite joy is within you.

No past, no future. Only now.

Enjoy today.

Don't worry about your life.

I'm taking care of you.

Don't be concerned about what you'll eat or wear.

I know what you need and I provide it.

Keep your mind on the mystery of your oneness with me.

Keep it simple, and be full of joy.

Luke 12:32-34 Luke 9:3 Luke 12:13-21 Psalm 118:24 Luke 18:18-25 Matthew 6:26 Matthew 6:24-34 John 15:11

Chapter 5 - Be Peaceful

Being joyful and being peaceful are closely related. Both are fruits of my spirit.

In the midst of what seems like chaos around you -- my peace within.

When storms swirl through your psyche, pause and put your trust in me.

I calm the raging sea.

I've given you my peace. You have it. It's yours.

My peace is within you.

My peace isn't based on circumstances.

There's nothing to worry about.

In me, you have life and peace.

Keep your mind on me and trust me, and I'll keep you in perfect peace.

Everything's unfolding perfectly.

My peace is beyond human reasoning.

Let my peace rule you.

Your peacefulness affects others. It brings joy to you and to them.

Live with peace and joy.

Galatians 5:22   Luke 5:16   Matthew 8:23-27   John 14:27
John 16:33   Luke 12:25-26   Romans 8:6   Isaiah 26:3
Philippians 4:7 Proverbs 12:20

Chapter 6 - Be Free

To be joyful, know that, in me, you're free.

There's a freedom more vast than the sky, when you let the notions of your ego die.

I don't condemn you. I set you free!

Live in freedom.

In the awareness of your oneness with me, you're free!

You're free of judging others.

You're free of caring how others judge you.

You're free of judging your self.

You're free of regret.

You're free of resentment.

You're free to be at peace in the present.

You're free of caring whether you lose or save face.

You're free -- because of my grace.

You're free because of my spirit within you.

During your experience as a human on earth, delight in the wonderful things I provide. Your home is in heaven. You're on a brief journey. Enjoy the ride!

My spirit is within you and it's everywhere.

Where my spirit is, there's freedom.

Luke 4:18 Romans 8:1 Galatians 5:1 John 8:32 John 8:36

Mark 8:34 Luke 6:36-38 Romans 15:7 Ecclesiastes 3:1-12

2 Corinthians 3:17

Chapter 7 - Love Others As I Love You

To be joyful, know that I love you, and love others as I love you.

There's nothing you could do that would stop me from loving you.

I love everything and everyone.

In love, you live in me and I live in you.

Forgetting about 'me and mine,' you have a joyful mind.

You're a transparency through which my love shines.

Keep your mind on things above, and do everything in love.

You're a conduit through which my love flows.

Be kind to your fellow humans. Everyone is struggling with something.

In the awareness of my love for you, bring that love to everything you do.

Know that you're loved and blessed, and sing with joy!

Psalm 118:1 1 John 4:16 1 Corinthians 16:14 Colossians 3:2
John 15:12 Psalm 59:16

Chapter 8 - Be Unattached

To be joyful, be unattached.

Be unattached to people, things, situations and outcomes.

Lose your life and find your life in me.

Trusting in me is the foundation of holy non-attachment.

I will only what's best for you.

Everything that happens or doesn't happen is for your good.

Be content, no matter what's going on.

It doesn't matter if people like you or if they don't like you.

Don't judge others, and don't be concerned about how others judge you. Don't even judge yourself.

It's not your job to 'fix,' change or 'rescue' anyone. Leave that to me. I'm working within everyone.

Accept others as I've accepted you.

Just be who you are.

You are who I made you to be, and I love you -- unconditionally.

This instant -- be born anew.

Look at everything from a cosmic view.

See! I'm making everything new.

Matthew 10:38 Proverbs 16:20 Romans 12:8 Luke 10:5-6
Luke 8:8-11 Romans 8:28 1 Corinthians 4:3 Psalm 139:1-3
Psalm 139:13-14 John 4:9 Revelation 21:5

Chapter 9 - Die to Your Self

To be joyful, die to your self.

Whatever happens is my perfect will for you.

You don't need to understand my will. Just trust it.

My will is done regardless of your attitude, so, in faith, welcome it with gratitude.

Become nothing -- and discover who you are.

I'm the only thing that's real.

Apart from me, you're powerless.

Turn everything over to me and discover the power of my grace.

Let go and let me.

Die daily. Before long -- you'll be gone!

Luke 22:42 Mark 8:34 John 3:1-6 John 14:6 Ephesians 4:32 2 Corinthians 12:9 Acts 14:22 1 Corinthians 15:31

Chapter 10 - Use Words Wisely

To be joyful, use words wisely.

Be thoughtful and considerate when speaking.

For the most part, keep silent.

Simply say yes when you mean yes and no when you mean no.

Don't talk much about your spiritual experiences. They're beyond words anyway.

Harsh words stir up anger, but gentle words are calming.

Don't complain or gossip.

Speak kindly about others.

Use words to encourage and inspire.

Kind words bring joy.

Proverbs 17:28 Proverbs 18:2 Matthew 5:37 Matthew 7:6
Matthew 2:1-21 Luke 2:39 Matthew 16:20 Mark 5:43 John
2:1-4 Proverbs 17:1 1 Peter 3:10 Ephesians 4:29

Chapter 11 - Be in My Kingdom

To be joyful, be in my kingdom.

My kingdom, -- 'the kingdom of God, the kingdom of heaven,' -- is within you.   It's a state of consciousness that transcends thoughts and words.

My kingdom is not of this world.

My kingdom is a state of being.   It's knowing that you're nothing and that I'm everything.

In my kingdom -- you live by faith, not by appearances.

Become like a little child.

Live as a child of light.

Be still -- and know me.

In the awareness of your oneness with me, you're in my kingdom.

You're a channel through which joy flows to everyone.

In my kingdom is boundless joy.

Luke 17:21 Matthew 13:44 1 Corinthians 1:20 John 18:36
2 Corinthians 5:7 Matthew 18:3 Ephesians 5:8 Matthew
5:14-16 Psalm 46:10 Romans 14:17

Chapter 12 - Be Conscious of My Presence

To be joyful, be conscious of my presence.

I'm in all creation. I shine from the sun and from the eyes of a child.

I'm the invisible essence of all that is.

I'm in everything -- and I'm beyond everything too.

I'm transcendent and immanent. I'm over all, through all and in all. It's all me!

I'm all, and in all. All means all. There's nothing that isn't me. There isn't me and something else. There's only me. I'm the "I" of every one. I'm the 'IS" of all that is. All that is -- is me!

I'm everywhere -- and I'm in you. And in me, you're everywhere too!

You're in me, and I'm in you.

You're a means through which I'm expressing myself.

I'm present in every situation.

In the awareness of my presence you have inexpressible joy.

Isaiah 6:3   Ephesians 4:6   Colossians 3:11   Jeremiah 23:24
John 14:20   Psalm 16:11

Chapter 13 - Trust in Me

To be joyful, trust in me.

I know what's best -- for you and for others.

I don't need your suggestions or your advice.

Trust in me and be with me in paradise.

I'm guiding you.

I'm making the path ahead straight and smooth.

Trust in me completely and rejoice!

Consider the Blessed Virgin Mary. Her faithful submission to
my will produced in her a profound joy.

Entrust everything to me.

Move the veil aside and see me -- the one and only Reality.

Trust in me and be joyful.

2 Corinthians 1:9 Isaiah 55:8-9 Luke 23:42-43 Psalm 13:5
Proverbs 3:5-6 John 14:1 Luke 1:38 Luke 1:47 Psalm 37:5
Genesis 28:16 2 Corinthians 3:16 John 7:24 Joshua 1:9
Psalm 28:7

Chapter 14 - Totally Surrender

To be joyful, totally surrender your will and your life to me.

Apart from me, you can't do anything.

Get out of the way. I'll handle it.

Within and without, leave everything to me.

My perfect will is revealed in all that's occurring.

Make a decision, right now, to turn your life over to me.

I'm transforming you. I'm setting you free.

You've surrendered your will and your life to me.

You now have a new way of seeing.

You're a new creation! You're a new being!

My joy is within you. Nothing and no one can take it away.

I love you with an infinite and everlasting love.

Be joyful always.

Delight in the wonderful mystery of it all.

John 15:5   John 14:1   Luke 23:46   2 Corinthians 12:9
Ephesians 3:12   2 Corinthians 3:17   John 8:36   Philippians
2:13 Psalm 119:35-36 2 Corinthians 5:17 John 16:22 Psalm
136:1 1 Thessalonians 5:16

Amen.

Thank you for reading Peace and Joy

This book is available from Amazon.com and other retailers. It is also available on Kindle and other devices.

If you have a question or a comment, my email address is:

sjcurran100@hotmail.com

Peace and joy be with you -- now and always.